mommy

please

talk

to me

Personal Grooming Tips
for Teenage Girls

PATRICE M. ELLIS

Mommy, Please Talk To Me

(This is a revised and expanded version of the original text, 'Personal Grooming Tips for Teenage Girls')

By Patrice M. Ellis

Printed in the United States of America

ISBN 978-1-60266-223-0

Cover Design & Layout by:
Nakeisha Nicolls
www.marlonicolls.com

www.xulonpress.com

mommy PLEASE talk to me

Personal Grooming Tips
for Teenage Girls

Foreword

I am extremely delighted that my life's partner and friend is moving closer and closer into the fulfillment of her divine assignment in life: to see to it that women in general and saved women in particular become women of excellence and elegance.

Patrice is anointed to do what she does and be who she is. How do I know? I have lived with her for almost three decades. What better way to produce women of excellence and elegance than to sow the seed while they are still children and teenagers? This work is geared toward teens. I sincerely believe that if the information in this book is adhered to, the readers will certainly grow up to become women of excellence and elegance.

I give God the praise for raising Patrice up with this assignment and I salute my wife and friend for being faithful to it.

✝ Neil C. Ellis

Dedication

This book is dedicated to my teenage daughter Renechea whom the Lord has given me the privilege to raise. She has, in her own way, helped me to understand the challenges of growing up in the early days of the 21st century.

I would only hope that the strong desire I now see in her to improve and enhance her life will continue until she becomes the strong Godly woman I know she can be: a woman of faith, determination, grace and class.

MOM

Table of Contents

Foreword 4

Dedication 5

Chapter 1 ......Head & Hair 10

Chapter 2 ......Face 14

Chapter 3 ......Underarm 18

Chapter 4 ......Hands 22

Chapter 5 ......Pubic Area 24

Chapter 6 ......Checkpoints Before Leaving Home....30

Chapter 7 ......Areas for Improvement 34

Chapter 8 ......Eating & Table Manners 38

Chapter 9 ......What Should You Do? 46

Chapter 10 ....Making a Good Impression 54

Chapter 11 ....Friendship Problems 76

Chapter 12 ....Dating 92

Introduction

Hi Girls,

I guess it's appropriate to say that you have more independence now that you are getting older. Of course this comes with more responsibility.

I'm sure that you are struggling because there are times that people expect you to function like an adult, but you are still feeling like a child. Wow! This is not easy for you.

Need some help? Here we go. Maybe giving you some guidelines for taking better care of yourself and getting along with other people might help you. A girl with good manners usually gets respect, because she's giving it.

Reading this book will give you the tools to handle certain situations, thereby finding confidence in yourself that you never thought you had.

Read, enjoy and share with a friend.

CHAPTER 1

HEAD & HAIR

Head & Hair

- You should have your hair washed and treated at least once a month. Every two (2) weeks is ideal (preferred) if it is affordable, unless you have the type of hair that can be washed daily.

- Oil/grease your scalp adequately so as to prevent dandruff and any other disorder caused by dry scalp.

- Try to avoid hot curling your hair every day as this will damage and eventually break the hair.

- Avoid the excessive use of gels as this causes unsightly build up, dryness of the hair and scalp and eventual breakage.

- Hairstyles that allow you to brush and comb your hair daily are preferred, because they allow your scalp to be stimulated, thus, causing your hair to grow.

- Be sure to have your hair tidy before leaving your room even if you are staying home.

- Avoid the usage of rubberbands over a long period of time. This too will cause hair breakage.

- Try not to over-process (relax) your hair. Hair should be relaxed every twelve (12) weeks unless there is tremendous new growth.

- Short hair requires more time to manage, so prepare to get up earlier in the mornings or see how much of what you need to do can be done at night.

- Stop rushing and put yourself together properly.

REMEMBER! You can wear nice clothes, fancy shoes, and great accessories (jewelry), but if your hair is not well groomed and tidy, then you don't look so well put together after all.

CHAPTER 2

FACE

Face

- Make sure that your face is washed thoroughly each morning before leaving home.

- Make sure that your face is thoroughly washed each evening before retiring for the day.

- If you are not going out, still wash your face thoroughly. (It just looks better when it's clean.)

- Check your face before leaving your room or bathroom.

- Make sure there is no soap remaining around your hairline.

- Remove all mucus build-up from your eyes.

- Make sure there is no 'snot', 'booga', or mucus in your nostrils.

- Check for drool marks around the mouth. A whole lot of people drool, and dribble at night. (LOL!)

- Of course, be sure to brush your teeth and tongue, and don't forget to floss.

- Gargle with mouth wash and make sure to remove any toothpaste from around your mouth.

- Makeup should be worn in moderation if it is allowed at all by your parents. Please consult with your parents before attempting.

- If you are experiencing acne, ask your parents to take you to a dermatologist, unless you have had success with over the counter medication.

- Do not spoil / ruin your face by using harsh chemicals or products on it too soon.

CHAPTER 3

UNDERARM

underarm

It is important that you wash under your arms (armpits) thoroughly before putting on your deodorant or antiperspirant. Remember that your body chemistry is changing, so a lot more care has to be taken with your body parts.

- Be sure to wash your underarm with lots of soap and water.

- Be sure to use an effective deodorant or antiperspirant.

- If your parents allow, keep your armpits shaven.

- Do not put deodorant under a dirty armpit.

- If you sweat a lot under your arms, be careful with the type of fabric your clothing is made of. *Note: some fabrics make you perspire (sweat) more than others. Natural fabrics like cotton are best.*

- You might need to take a towel and soap with you to school if your body odor is very strong (offensive) and you can't wait until bath time.

- Be sure to take soap, deodorant and/or antiperspirant on the day that you have physical education at school.

- Do not put spray deodorant on a freshly shaven armpit; it will burn. Use a solid deodorant for a few days and test under your arm before you resume the use of your regular spray deodorant.

- When I was growing up, my grandmother used to say to me that by the time you smell yourself, others have already smelt you. I didn't like her saying that, but now that I am older, might I say that I do agree.

CHAPTER 4

HANDS

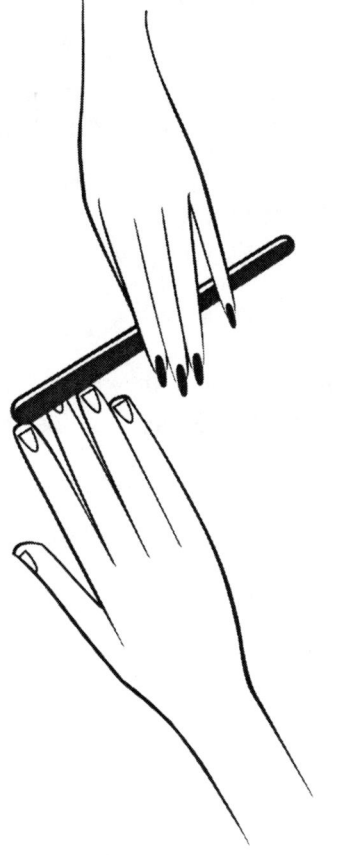

Hands

- Keep them clean at all times.

- Keep your nails clean and cut to a moderate length. (It just looks more classy).

- If you must do all the nail painting, keep it moderate and with mild colors, because you do not want to draw attention to yourself or look like you have claws instead of fingernails.

- The french manicures are very appropriate for teenagers, because it has a classic and clean look.

- In choosing this look, however, make sure that you select the shade that is best for your skin tone.

- You do not need an excessive amount of jewelry.

REMEMBER! Simple is **always** classic and elegant.

CHAPTER 5

PUBIC AREA

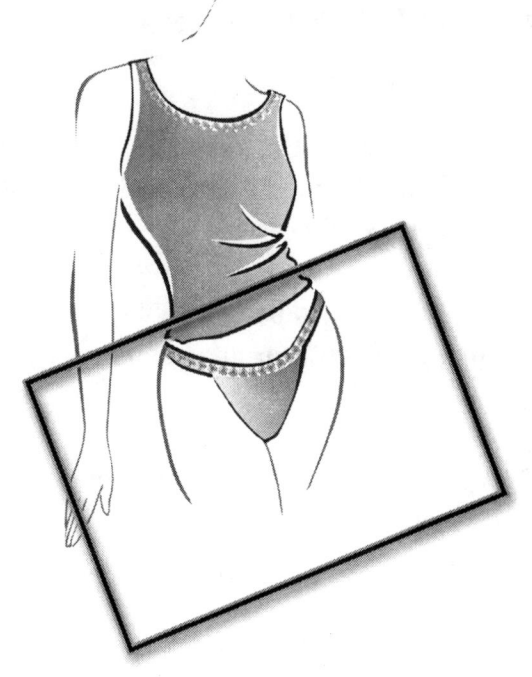

Pubic Area

This is a touchy area and a subject that is very uncomfortable for a whole lot of people, but here goes. I cannot explain to you sufficiently the importance of keeping this area clean.

- Be sure to wear clean underwear (panties) every morning and evening, after you have taken a bath.

- A panty shield helps to keep the panty fresh and clean.

- Be sure to clean the inner lips of the vagina (labia minora and majora) and not just wash the outside (surface).

- More care need to be taken during the time of the month when you are having your menses (period, monthly).

- Don't forget to let your mother know each month when your period comes.

- Please observe and let your mom know the volume (amount) of the period and the color, i.e. Whether the flow is bright red or dark red.

- Let her know how many pads you are having to change per day.

- Let her know if there are any clots on the pad or otherwise, e.g. When you go to pass your urine, do you feel clumps of blood dropping out in the toilet?

- Let her know how many pairs of panties you are changing, or whether you are soiling your bed linen, i.e. if your period is too heavy/and or is accompanied by clots and, in some cases, pain, it could be an indication of some gynecological problem.

- Dispose of your sanitary pads properly. (Do not just throw them in the garbage). Wrap them in the wrapper or newspaper before throwing them away.

- Be sure to wash your hands after you have changed your pad.

- Tampons are not encouraged until you are more mature, as they can cause infections, etc.

- Panty shields should be worn otherwise to prevent your panties from becoming soiled.

- Remember to also dispose of these properly.

- Let your mom know if there is any abnormal discharge or secretions, i.e. Any discharge that is green, yellow, brown, and certainly anything that has an odor, would need to be checked and treated if necessary.

- Be sure and let your mom know if you are experiencing any physical discomfort, e.g. abdominal pain, vomiting or any other symptoms.

- Dark underwear during the time of your period is always preferred in case of soiling, and do not wear very light colored outer clothing during this time of the month.

- Soiled underwear should be washed and hung to dry before being placed in the dirty clothes hamper.

- Your period is a personal matter and should not be broadcasted (told) to everyone.

- Change your sanitary pad as often as is necessary, for your comfort and to avoid leakage on to your underwear, as well as to eliminate odor.

MOMMY PLEASE TALK TO ME

- Panty shields should be worn on lighter days and continued when you are not having your period to avoid your panties becoming soiled from regular vaginal secretions.

- Some of you may have long pubic hair. If it is tangling or getting caught in your underwear, you might want to trim (cut) it lower.

- Douching is a personal thing and people do it for all kinds of reasons, but know that this is not a procedure that is necessary at anytime, because God has designed the body so that it has its own way of getting rid of anything that does not need to be there.

REMEMBER! Other people smell you before you smell yourself. STAY PLEASANTLY CLEAN.

CHAPTER 6

CHECKPOINTS BEFORE LEAVING HOME

wash face ✓

brush teeth ✓

bathe ✓

look at self in mirror ✓

double check yourself ✓

Checkpoints Before Leaving Home

- Look in the mirror at yourself or ask someone to inspect you before you leave your home or wherever.

- Make sure that you are wearing lotion and deodorant.

- Make sure that you are appropriately dressed for the occasion.

- Make sure that you are wearing the appropriate undergarments (size and color).

- Make sure that your clothes are not too tight or too short.

- Your armpits are considered private (it grows hair) so they should not be exposed everywhere.

- Be sure that you wear clothes that are appropriate for you based upon your age, size and the occasion.

- Ensure that your undergarments are not visible through your clothing.

- Make sure that your clothes are not torn anywhere. (I know that young people can get very lazy).

- Make sure that all buttons are sewn on properly.

- Make sure that your clothes and shoes are clean.

- Most people make sure that their hair is fixed and their nails and done, but neglect other areas.

- Make sure that your breasts are not exposed to the public.

REMEMBER! Your fragrance (perfume) should be mild: not too overpowering.

CHAPTER 7

AREAS FOR IMPROVEMENT

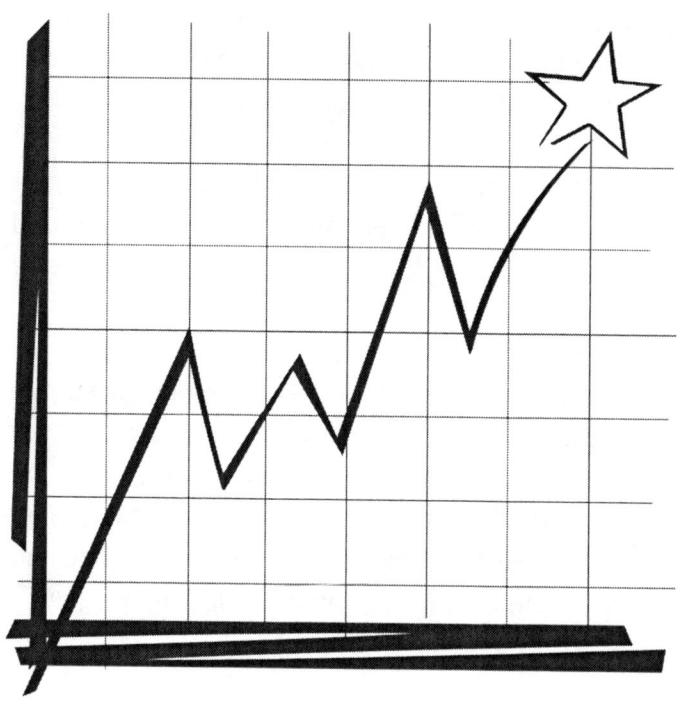

Areas for Improvement

- Put dirty clothes in the hamper, not in the drawers.

- Hang clothes up properly in the closet or place in the drawer when you are finished with them.

- Clothes should not be placed under the bed, on the bed, on the floor, or on the chair in your room, neither on the dresser drawer.

- Dirty clothes should not be worn at anytime. I am particularly referring to bras, camisoles and socks.

- Buy less trendy clothes and focus more on classic fashions. It does not matter what the latest fashion is, neither does it matter what the sales person says, they (sales persons) work on commission (they get paid for every sale they make). Buy clothes that suit your shape, size and age. Remember that not every style is for you.

- Sleep in P.J.'s and not day clothes, warm-up suits, exercise gear and/or big tee shirts. Practice being a young lady because that is what you are. Prepare for your life's partner.

- Be sure to take a robe if you are sleeping over at a friend's house.

- After your body parts are fully developed, you should not walk around your house in your underwear unless it is in the privacy of your room.

- Stay away from the tomboy look.

- Be attractive and feminine.

- Sexy is not naked. Wear clothes that are becoming of a young lady.

- Stop leaving urine in the toilet (commode). Flush the toilet after each use.

- When you're having your period, be sure to flush the toilet after usage and clean up any mess left behind.

- Of course, wash your hands after using the toilet.

- Be sure to take a bath immediately after you get home from school, before getting into any activity, especially if you have younger siblings (brothers and sisters) and you play with them after you get home.

- Certainly be sure to wash your hands before cooking or the preparation of any food items.

- No scratching of body parts during food preparation.

- Pull your hair back in a ponytail when cooking or wear a hair net.

- Do not taste the food from the cooking spoon. Put a sample in your hand then taste.

- When making tea, lemonade or any soft drink, do not sample by putting the spoon in your mouth. Again, drop a sample in your hand for tasting.

- Learn to eat healthy and sensibly. Cut back on fast food.

CHAPTER 8

EATING
&
TABLE
MANNERS

Eating & Table Manners

Knowing how to share and being considerate of others, make mealtimes more pleasant at home, and is one of the first things people notice about you when you are their guest.

Table manners are very important, because they remind us how to share and how to be considerate of others.

WHEN TO START

- If you are at home, sit down when you are called and put your napkin in your lap, but wait for everyone to be seated before you start to eat.

- If you are a guest, wait for the hostess to start eating before you begin.

- If the food is out on the table, (buffet style) take the item nearest to you and put it on your plate.

- If the dish is a big one, help the person next to you by holding it while he / she serve themselves.

WHAT TO DO & WHAT NOT TO DO

- Always pass the food to the right if persons are helping themselves.

- When at home and you want second helpings, just ask, but if you are a guest at someone's home, wait for them to offer seconds if there is enough food.

- Do not reach across the table. If you would like something, ask for it e.g. *"May I have the bread please?"*

- Always chew with your mouth closed.

- Do not talk while you eat. The sight of chewed food is disgusting.

- Do not blow bubbles in your drink or make objects with your mashed potatoes. This says that you would rather play with your food.

Position for the utensils while at rest.

Hold the knife and fork like this, not in your fists.

- Cut small pieces of meat at a time and eat.

- No slurping at the table, especially through a straw.

- No eating ice at the table.

- Do not pick your teeth at the table.

- Do not clean your teeth with your napkin at the table.

- Do not blow your nose at the table.

- Do not push your food onto your fork with your finger; use the knife.

- Do not order things from the menu that you will not eat.

- Do not order or take up food just because it is available.

- Do not put salt on your food before tasting it, especially at someone's residence, (this can be offensive.)

- Do not push your plate away when you are finished.

-
  Position for knife and fork when you are finished.

- Never put your butter directly on your bread. Put butter first on your dinner or bread plate.

- If someone uses your bread plate, simply use the side of your dinner plate for your bread.

- Never spit fish or chicken bone directly on to your plate. Always place it on the fork first, and discard it on the left side of the food you are eating.

- If you notice someone taking a tablet at the table, do not ask what it is for.

- Keys, cell phones, purses, shades etc. are not to be placed on the dinner table.

- Pay attention to the people sitting around you and see what kind of conversation you can get going.

- Do not burp out loud.

- Try not to belch at the table, but if you do, simply say, "Excuse me," but not to anyone in particular.

- Do not lean back in the chair on its back legs.

- Keep elbows off the table (*you appear lazy and bored*), and no slouching please.

- Do not freshen up your lip gloss at the table.

- Do not wipe your lipstick or lip gloss off with the napkin. Simply pat your mouth gently if you must wipe at all.

- Please do not pack up the balance of your meal in foil paper and put it in your handbag to take home. (*Doggy bag*).

CHAPTER 9

WHAT SHOULD YOU DO?

What should you do?

YOU ARE OVER AT A FRIEND'S HOUSE AND IT IS JUST ABOUT DINNER TIME. WHAT DO YOU DO?

- Wash your hands, and check in the kitchen with the parent to see if there is something you can help with.

- Pour drinks or water, set the table, take out the ketchup or salad dressing etc. These are just a few things that you can do.

- This posture is even good at home. I'm sure that your mom will appreciate it.

- Do not take your cue from your friend in this instance. Remember, she lives there.

AS SOON AS YOUR FOOD IS PLACED BEFORE YOU, YOU REALIZE THAT YOU REALLY HAVE TO GO TO THE BATHROOM:

- Say, "May I be excused for a moment, please?" and go.

- Place your napkin on the chair when you get up to go.

YOU ARE OFFERED A FOOD ITEM THAT YOU ARE ALLERGIC TO:

- Say, "No thank you. I am allergic to that particular food." Or just say, "No thank you."

- Make a meal out of the other food items on the table or on your plate.

IF YOUR FORK DROPS:

- Ask for a clean one if you are in a restaurant.

- If at a friend's house, pick up the fork and say that you dropped it. That's time for your friend to get you a new one.

YOUR DRINK SPILLS ON THE TABLE-CLOTH:

- Say, "I'm sorry" in a genuine way.

- Help to clean it up.

- Say you're sorry again when you are leaving.

- Tell your parents when you get home. They may want to also apologize to the host.

- Don't be embarrassed. Tell yourself, "Accidents happen to everyone, even adults."

- If you apologize sincerely, and do whatever is necessary, most people will forgive you and not worry about it anymore.

A PIECE OF HAIR OR BUG IS IN YOUR FOOD:

- Ask for another plate. Explain if you have to, but do not make a scene.

- Do not intentionally put bugs or hair in your food while out, so that you can get another serving.

MOMMY PLEASE TALK TO ME

YOU BELCH AT THE TABLE:

- Say, "Excuse me," (but to no one in particular).

IF SOMEONE AT THE TABLE TAKES A PILL:

- Don't ask what the pill is for.

- Better yet, if you need to take medicine at the table, just take it and do not comment. Of course, it is better to do this before coming to the table.

YOU'RE EATING FISH OR CHICKEN, AND YOU WANT TO SPIT OUT THE BONE:

- Do not just spit it out on the plate.

- Put it on the fork and then place it on the left side of the food item that you are eating.

YOU WANT TO TAKE SOME BUTTER FROM THE BUTTER DISH:

- Using a clean utensil, remove the piece of butter that you want and rest it on your bread plate (preferably) or on your dinner plate.

- Never use your hand unless the butter is individually wrapped.

- Do not put it directly on the bread.

YOU ARE AT A FUNCTION AND THE TABLE IS SET WITH GLASSES FOR WINE:

- Identify the glasses for the various drinks and turn down the ones that you do not plan to use.

IF A PIECE OF MEAT OR FOOD PARTICLE IS STUCK IN YOUR TEETH:

- Use your tongue discreetly to try and dislodge it. If this fails, go to the bathroom and do whatever is necessary to get the food out.

- If something is stuck in your friend's teeth, let her know by gesturing with a small hand motion; don't wait for her to discover it. She may not be aware.

- Remember, be a good friend, and "do unto others as you would have them do unto you."

IMPORTANT

At formal dinners, all of the food is not served at once. Please note that food is brought to you. You eat and then your plate is removed and replaced with another dish.

Each part of the meal is termed a 'course'. Do not take large portions, but do try everything. It's okay if you don't eat everything on your plate.

At a really formal dinner, you may have up to five courses or more with a menu to list them.

You may even have more silverware than you expect. If you do not know what utensil to use for the different courses, watch your host.

CLUE:

If in doubt, always use the silverware furthest from your plate first, and then move inward.

DIAGRAM OF A FORMAL TABLE SETTING

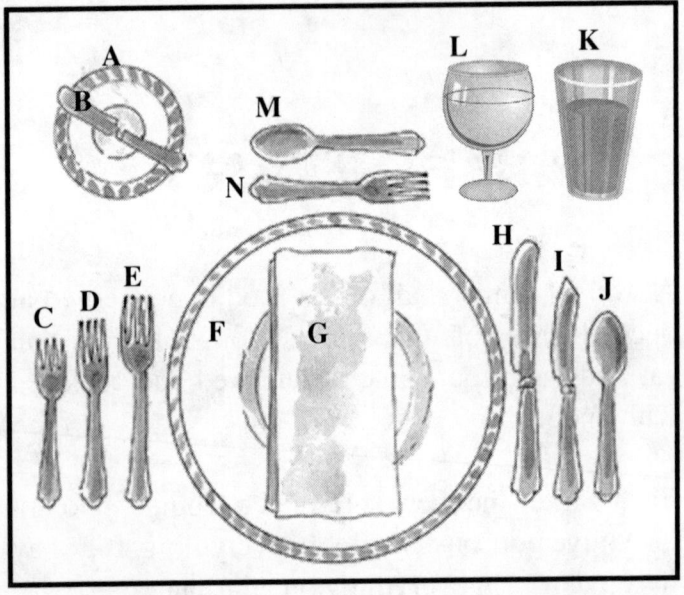

A- Butter Plate
B- Butter Knife
C- Salad Fork
D- Fish Fork
E- Dinner Fork
F- Service Plate
G- Napkin

H- Dinner Knife
I- Fish Knife
J- Soup Spoon
K- Soft Drink Glass
L- Water Glass
M-Dessert Spoon
N-Dessert Fork

MOMMY PLEASE TALK TO ME

CHAPTER 10

MAKING A GOOD IMPRESSION

Making a Good Impression

How many times have you heard the phrase "do not judge a book by its cover"? Isn't it interesting, though, that as often as we are told not to do this, we continue to make judgement about others based on how they look and how they speak?

This kind of posture is very unfair to persons that you will meet and sometimes causes you to lose out on what could have been a wonderful relationship. Yet making a good first impression is still very important.

The more you practice these tips, the more natural they will seem and the more confident you will become.

ALWAYS STAND TALL:

- Your posture says a lot about what you think about yourself.

- Put your shoulders back.

54

- Hold your head up high.

- Speak intelligently and in a strong, confident voice.

- Don't cover your mouth when you speak.

- Walk with confidence and you will begin to feel confident. Then others will begin to see you the same way.

WHEN MEETING PEOPLE:

- Always make eye contact.

- Look people in the face. It says that you are honest and are interested in what the person is saying.

- If you are shy, look in the safety zone which is the space in between the eyebrows.

- Greet people by their name where possible. (People like this. It makes them feel good and it shows that you care.)

- Say "hello". "Hi" means I know you very well and I'm glad to see you.

- Stand and shake hands when you are saying hello to an adult, especially if it is a formal setting. Offer your right hand even if you are left handed.

- Hold doors for adults.

- If you and a friend are going through a doorway, let her go ahead of you.

- If you are on a crowded bus or in a crowded building, give up your seat to someone who needs it more. This includes older people and people with babies or small children.

- Always stand when an adult guest comes into the room.

- Always use the magic words "please" and "thank you". (You will almost always get cooperation and a smile.)

- Words like "duh" should only be used with your friends. Adults can find it insulting and a child who does not know you might feel hurt if spoken to in this way.

- Pleasant words do not count if not said in a pleasant tone. E.g. To yell "I'm sorry" almost seems like you're not sorry.

MOMMY PLEASE TALK TO ME

- Curse words are not necessary. There are thousands of better words in the English language to choose from.

- The more respect you show for yourself and the more you give, the more you get.

POSTURE

- Your posture sends a message to onlookers.

- You should look confident.

- You should look comfortable.

- You should give off the appearance of grace.

- Your posture plays a very important part in how you carry (wear) your clothes.

STANDING

- When standing, you should stand erect, either with one foot pivoting at an angle, or just straight with both feet together.

- You should feel comfortable, not strained.

- Your shoes should be comfortable in size and the appropriate height for your age.

- Your hands should hang loosely at your side.

- You should not be fidgeting with your clothes, nor put your hands in your mouth, or have them crisscrossed in front of you.

- Your shoulders should be erect and your chin up.

- Never stand with your legs spread apart. It draws negative attention.

WALKING

- Walk with grace and confidence.

- Try to walk in a straight line, with your shoulders erect, head and chin up.

- Practice walking with a book balanced on your head in a straight line.

- When walking up and down the stairs, do not run or skip.

- Turn your body slightly to the side and descend or ascend the steps sideways, so as not to trip over.

SITTING

- Stand in front of your chair.

- Make sure that you feel the chair with the back of your calves.

- Bend your knees as you lower your bottom onto the chair.

- Place one hand on each side of the seat and slide your bottom in the chair until your bottom touches the back of the chair.

- Your back should be erect. No slouching or leaning forward.

- Your legs should be placed flat-footed in front of you, crossed at the ankle.

- Your hand should rest comfortably in your lap.

- Do not cross your leg at the knee.

- Always keep your legs closed. (No one wants to see your undergarment.)

GETTING UP FROM YOUR CHAIR

- Be poised.

- Uncross your legs if they are crossed.

- Slide them inward toward the chair.

- Use your hands as support.

- Place them on your lap or on the seat and push yourself up.

GETTING IN & OUT OF THE CAR

- Open the car door.

- Rest your bottom (hip) on the seat with your legs still on the outside.

- Take a hold of the handle that is situated above the seat in the roof of the car.

- Hold firm, lift your legs and swing them inside the car.

60

TELEPHONE MANNERS

- Try not to call a person's house before nine o'clock in the morning or after ten o'clock at night even though your friend may be awake.

- Always identify yourself to the person who answers the phone.

- Always be polite.

- If the phone call is not for you, ask the caller if they can hold on please.

- If the caller says yes, go and find the person and do not yell to them from where you are.

- Cover the mouth of the receiver if you are going to yell so that the caller does not hear this.

- If for some reason the person cannot be found, ask if you can take a message.

- Some families prefer you to identify the family when answering the phone, but hello is quite fine.

- When calling someone's home, always acknowledge the person on the other end before asking for your party.

- When on the phone you should be paying attention to the person on the other end and not distracted by other things e.g. eating, watching TV, etc.

- If there is an incoming call for your parents or a family member, ask your friend if it's okay to call them back.

- If you dialed the wrong number, simply say "I'm sorry, I think I've dialed the wrong number."

- Don't just hang up; that's rude.

- Check to make sure you have the right number before dialing again.

- If you are answering the phone and someone has dialed the wrong number, simply ask the caller what number they are trying to reach.

- If the number the caller gives is not yours, say so, but if it is, simply say "It's the correct number, but no one lives here by that name."

- Do not answer questions like, "Are you home alone?"

USAGE OF THE CELL PHONE

- Be considerate of those around you. The world does not want to be a part of your phone call.

- Find a place away from people to have your conversation.

- Turn your ringer off in places where it can disturb others or the event that's going on.

- Don't get so caught up talking to people who aren't there until you ignore the people who are there.

- If you are leaving a message on a voice mail or answering service, keep it short. This is a recording, not a conversation.

- Cell phones are a convenience and are really used for emergency. Don't abuse it, so that you don't spend more money on the bill than you have to.

SLEEPOVERS OR BEING AT A FRIEND'S HOUSE

- Getting together with friends is always fun, but there are some guidelines to remember; each household is different and has its own habits and rules.

- If you are the host, always greet your guest at the door.

- If you are invited over, pitch in and fit in.

- Introduce your friend to your family if she has never been over to your house

- Make her feel welcome. Offer her something to drink and eat.

- Give your friend any info that she may need to know e.g. Your dad's study is off limit and so is your parents' bedroom.

- Be flexible when choosing what you will do. Ask your friend's opinion.

- Respect the belongings of people in the house.

- Don't wander around snooping on your own. Let your friend be your guide.

- Snooping around is wrong. Don't open cupboards or inspect closets.

- Never read a person's mail even if it is left open on the counter.

- Be friendly to other people in the house.

- If you need to use the phone or anything for that matter, ask first.

- Never help yourself to food or any other item. Always ask.

- If you make a mess, help clean it up.

- Strip or make your bed before you leave.

- Use good manners at the table and clean your place when you've finished eating.

- Help your friend with any chores that she may have.

- If you are feeling home-sick or ill, it's okay to talk to your friend or her parents.

- Change your clothes in the bathroom if you want to be alone.

- Be sure to take your house coat with you always so that you do not expose yourself.

- Don't stay too long in the bathroom, remember you are not at home.

- Make sure the bathroom is clean when you are finished.

- Rinse out the sink after you brush your teeth.

- Wipe up all the water off the counter & floor.

- Use only the towel you are told to use or are given.

- Fold the towel & hang it up when you are finished.

- Always say thank you when you are leaving.

- It would be nice to ask your parents if you can have your friend over in return.

- If they say yes, then for the most part, the same suggestions apply.

GOING TO THE MALL / MOVIES

Hey! Your parents are now allowing you a little free time on your own with your friends. You've got some money and you invite some of your friends to go with you.

Here are some of the things that you need to pay attention to and put into practice:

- Always let your parents know your whereabouts and who you are with, especially if they did not drop you off.

- Call when you reach your destination.

- If you have to change plans for some reason, be sure to call home so that your parents are not worried unnecessarily.

- Always be aware of your immediate surroundings.

- Do not take out all of your money at the same time.

- Secure your Credit Card, if you have one, and guard your PIN number.

- Do not put your handbag down anywhere unattended.

- Spend your money wisely.

- Do not be so busy talking and having fun that you are not aware of what is going on around you.

- Hold doors open for people carrying packages, parents with babies or anyone that looks as if they could use some assistance if they are in your vicinity.

- Say "Thank you," if someone holds the door for you.

- When you go to the movie, do not talk the movie that you are watching if you have already seen it. That could be annoying.

- Turn your cell phone off or put it on vibrate before going inside.

- Don't put your foot in / on the chair.

- Try not to block anyone's view.

- Don't throw popcorn or food on the floor.

- Don't jump the line at the refreshment counter.

- Don't allow anyone to touch you inappropriately. If this happens, yell "stop it" and yell it loud enough to get someone's attention.

- Let your parents know about the incident.

- Always stay with your group of friends. Do not separate.

- If you go into a store, and you are looking at an item, be sure to put it back on the right shelf, when you are done if you are not going to purchase it.

- Do not waste the salesperson's time if you have no intention of making a purchase.

- Cover each other. If one of you does something that is wrong or acts in a compromising manner, the rest of you should get on her case and discourage her from doing it.

- Do not allow your friends to cause you to get into trouble. Leave if you must.

GIFT GIVING / RECEIVING

Gifts are given for all kinds of reasons, but whenever they are given, it is a way of showing that you care. Gifts are also good to receive. Here are a few tips on the topic:

- Invitations to just about any event calls for a gift.

- Do not take a gift if the invitation says "no gift please."

- The gift should be appropriate, (something that can be used).

- It should be something that is useful or needed.

- Do not buy things such as toothpaste or mouthwash as gifts. That's insulting.

- Do not purchase a gift just to say you did.

- Make sure that it is something that you like, but buy it with the person in mind. i.e. buy a gift with the person's personality in mind.

- Wrap it nicely, not just in any old paper.

- Place a nice bow on it and a card with the person's name and a greeting.

- When you receive a gift, be sure to say "Thank you," perhaps with an expression, "How pretty," or "It's my favorite colour."

- If you can't find something nice to say about the gift, say something nice to the giver e.g. "How nice of you." Or "You're very kind."

- Another option is to call on the phone and say "Thank you."

- If you are writing a thank you note, make sure that the note is neat, not sloppy with misspelt words.

- Do re-read the note before you send it.

- If you get two or more of the same item, check to see if there is a tag, maybe you can exchange it for something else.

PROBLEM FOODS

When is the last time you wondered how to eat certain foods? Need a little help? Here we go...

BACON
   If it is crisp, you can eat it with your finger, otherwise use a knife and fork.

CAKE
   If it is bite size, feel free to eat it with your finger, but if it has sauce or is sticky or served with ice cream, then by all means use a fork and spoon with the fork serving as a pusher and the spoon as a scoop.

DIPS & CHIPS

Your dip should be taken from the container with a spoon or fork and placed on a plate along with the salsa and/or other side orders. Eat your chips with your fingers, and do not dip your chip in the main salsa container after you have bitten your chip.

TACOS

Use your hands for starters, then use a fork to get up all of the fillings from your plate that fell out earlier.

CHICKEN

Eat this with a knife and fork, unless you are at a picnic or a very casual affair. If visiting and in doubt, do what the hostess does.

BREAD

Bread should be placed on the little plate to the left of your dinner plate. It should be torn, not in half but in bite size pieces, one at a time. Butter each piece on it's own and eat.

BAKED POTATO

Cut the potato in half (length wise), push the potato inward from both ends and use a fork to mash in the butter, sour cream and any other item that you wish to use.

SPAGHETTI

Wind a few strands on your fork. Do not cut spaghetti strands with your knife.

SALAD

Cut your lettuce into small pieces before you start to eat, and watch out for cherry tomatoes. If you eat them whole they may squirt.

SOUP

Insert your spoon and move it away from you to the edge of the bowl. Rest the spoon on the edge of the bowl for a while, let it cool and then pour it in your mouth.

CHAPTER 11

FRIENDSHIP PROBLEMS

What Would You Do?

Friendship Problems

What would you do?

Making and keeping friends is not always easy. I am sure that friendships were easier to make when you were in kindergarten. For the most part, your parents decided who your friends were going to be and whenever you had a problem with them, your parents or some adult stepped in and made things better.

Now that you are older, a lot has changed. You are now choosing your own friends and you're trying to solve your own problems.

You're probably beginning to see that friendships are two-way streets and that means that both persons have to work at making the friendship a success.

No one person is "in charge". Each friendship is different. You value your friends for different reasons, e.g. one of them might make you laugh a lot when you're down, and another might give you good advice when you need to solve problems. At

MOMMY PLEASE TALK TO ME

the end of the day, I think every girl has what it takes to be a great friend and choose friends who are right for her.

SOME GIRLFRIEND CHALLENGES / POSSIBLE SOLUTIONS

JEALOUSY

This is not a good thing. Even though most of us at some point have felt a little jealous of someone for whatever reason, you need to deal with the feeling before it ruins the relationship.

Jealousy is a poison. What do you do if you find yourself in this position?

- Pray and ask God to remove that spirit from you.

- Admit that you are jealous. You can say "I'm happy for you but I'm feeling really jealous too."

- This helps your friend to know how you are feeling.

- Remember that no one has a perfect life.

- Everyone has a different strength, struggle and weakness.

- Look at your own life. What do you love that you wouldn't trade for anything?

- Know that some people have problems that you need to be happy you do not have.

- Be sensitive.

- Sharing your experiences is easier than bragging.

Challenge # 1
I have a friend who copies everything I do. It's annoying. What should I do?

- Maybe your friend admires you and your style.

- Maybe she's trying to see if it suits her.

- She's actually paying you a kind of compliment.

- Encourage her to come up with her own unique style by letting her know how special she is.

MOMMY PLEASE TALK TO ME

- Because you did something first doesn't mean it's exclusively yours.

- It just means you are a trendsetter.

Challenge # 2
I have a weird friend who eats off my plate. I do not want to hurt her feelings, but she's forcing me to. What should I do?

- Be honest with her.

- Talk to her alone and tell her how you feel when she eats off your plate.

- Sometimes when others know what annoys you, they can stop.

- If it doesn't stop, break off the relationship gently (if you can).

- Let her know you feel pressured by the relationship, and you want to spend time with other girls. Encourage her to do the same.

Challenge # 3

I called a friend some very offensive names. I tried apologizing, but nothing worked. Is there a way that I can make her forgive me?

- You cannot make anyone do what they do not want to do.

- All you can really do is admit that you were wrong and hope your friend remembers that everyone makes mistakes.

- Apologize.

- Give it time.

- Apologize again and make sure it's sincere.

- Say how angry you were, and how you wished you had handled the situation differently.

- Promise that you will never call them names again.

- Know that "Sorry," does not always fix things. Decide now to get a better grip on your anger.

Challenge # 4

My friend and I had a fight. We haven't spoken all summer and school is getting ready to re-open. I'm afraid. What should I do?

- Call her or write a note saying that you are sorry and give her an opportunity to say that she is also sorry.

- Do not use another friend as a 'go between'.

- Send her a note saying that you miss her and want to start over.

- Work this out yourself.

Challenge # 5

Your friend told a secret that you trusted her with and then lied about the fact that she did it. You feel hurt, angry and humiliated. What do you do?

- Ask yourself a few questions.

- How could someone who liked you and accepted you turn on you so quickly?

- Is this the only time that this is going to happen?

- Should I take her back?

- What if it happens again?

- What am I willing to go through for this friendship?

- What will it take for enough to be enough?

Challenge # 6
Your friend has been talking badly about you. You feel stabbed in the back. What should you do?

- Find a good time to talk one on one.

- Go to your friend and talk to her.

- Find out if it's true.

- Do it soon.

- Try not to involve others. It puts them in the middle and makes things confusing.

- If it is true, find out what's behind it.

MOMMY PLEASE TALK TO ME

- Ask for an apology if you feel you deserve one.

TALKING IT OUT / TIPS

When you and a friend get into a fight or argument; approach is very important. If you want to resolve things, do not back your friend up against the wall.

PAY ATTENTION TO THESE PHRASES AND THEIR MEANINGS...

1. "CAN WE TALK?"
   Says I want to resolve things.

2. "HOW DO YOU SEE WHAT HAPPENED?"
   Says that you know that she has a point of view and you're willing to hear it.

3. "REMEMBER THE OTHER DAY? WELL, IT'S BEEN BOTHERING ME. I WAS REALLY HURT..."
   Says that both of you can solve the problem together because they are being very specific.

4. "I DON'T GET WHAT YOU MEAN,
   COULD YOU EXPLAIN IT TO ME?"
   Says I'm trying to cut you some slack.

5. "MAYBE WE HAVE TO AGREE TO
   DISAGREE."
   Says, I respect your opinion and I'm willing
   to compromise to an extent, but I expect my
   opinion to be respected too.

6. "OUR FRIENDSHIP MEANS A LOT TO
   ME, AND I WANT TO WORK THIS OUT."
   Says I'm willing to do my part if you're willing
   to do yours.

- Pick a good time and place to talk.

- You need privacy.

- You need a lot of time to get anywhere with the
  conversation.

- Listen - hear what your friend has to say. She
  has feelings too.

- Talking on the phone is okay, but face to face is
  better.

- Writing is okay, but remember once you put
  something in writing, you cannot take it back.

- Plan what you will say. Remember, you are talking about your feeling, not your friend's shortcomings.

- Stick to how you feel about what happened, not what a rotten friend she's been.

- If you begin to attack her with accusations she will have to defend herself.

- Tell your friend what you want to happen to make things right, e.g. an apology, an explanation.

- Do you have something that you need to apologize for?

- If you do not resolve the situation, maybe you need to walk away, but you do not have to be enemies.

- Be honest but not hurtful.

- You can still say "Hi," when your paths cross, once you end the relationship.

- Do not go around talking badly about your friend. Remember you cannot take words back.

- Do not accommodate anyone talking about your friend.

- Try not to have an attitude with other people that still talk to that friend. Remember you cannot control people. They have a right to interact with whomever they choose.

HOW TO GIVE AN APOLOGY

- Be honest / sincere.

- Take responsibility for your actions.

- Be specific.

- Let your friend know how badly you feel about your part in the argument.

- Let her know what you think you should've done and what you will do the next time.

- Let her know that you value the relationship and will try not to let this happened again.

HOW TO RECEIVE AN APOLOGY: ADMITTING YOU'RE WRONG ISN'T EASY:

- Hear your friend out.

- Listen carefully to what she is saying.

- Don't relive the argument or things that have happened in the past.

- Accept her apology. This does not mean that you have forgiven her. It means that you understand that she feels badly about what happened.

- True forgiveness takes time and it takes time to regain trust in her as a friend again.

- Consider whether or not you also need to apologize for your part in the ordeal.

THE POPULARITY THING

THERE ARE TWO KINDS OF POPULAR:

1. The one where a person seems to have it altogether, but they know how to make others

feel good about themselves. Everyone wants to be around them, because people admire them.

2. The one that's based on power. They make people feel small and unimportant, and then they use this to get on top. They are feared. These are bullies.

FACES OF A BULLY:

The pretender:
Sweetly asks a question. Pretends to have your interest at heart but reports everything that you say differently e.g. "Hi Mary, what do you think about John?"
"He's nice."
Later the pretender reports, "Mary has a crush on John."

The intimidator:
Uses threats to gain power. "Do as I say or you'll be sorry!"

The harasser:
Everyday, they target certain people and abuse them by saying things like: "There's something on your face". When you wipe your face, they may say something like "You can't wipe off ugly".

MOMMY PLEASE TALK TO ME

The rule setter:

She makes the rules and decides who is in the group e.g. "Check out my girl today. Because you are not wearing our colors, you do not fit into our group."

WAYS TO DEAL WITH BULLIES:

1. Don't let her know that she has hurt you.

2. Roll your eyes, perhaps and walk away.

3. Pretend that you didn't hear anything, but if they persist, say something like "Really?   I didn't know that."

4. Laugh and say "whatever."

5. Say "If I valued your opinion, I would be offended by that."

6. Say "That wasn't very nice. How would you feel if I said that to you?"

7. Say, "That's your opinion, but it's not mine."

CHAPTER 12

DATING

Some Helpful Dating Tips

Dating

This is an exciting time in the life of a teenager, one I am sure you are looking forward to, but also a very critical (serious) time.

How soon you date has all to do with when your parents feel that you are responsible enough and can be trusted with a member of the opposite sex. Because you are now a teenager does not automatically mean anything.

Do not pay any attention to what is happening with your friends or what their parents are allowing them to do.

Can you date and still be focused? Can you date and abstain from sexual activity or actions that can lead to this kind of behaviour? Well, here are a few helpful hints:

- Your parents should speak with both you and your date about their expectations.

- Date in groups. This is safe and makes you accountable.

MOMMY PLEASE TALK TO ME

- Do not go off somewhere just the two of you, away from the group.

- Avoid places and environments that will cause your hormones to race.

- Avoid caressing and hugging and the kissing of any part of the body, including the lips.

- Keep your conversations clean i.e. not sexual.

- Do not watch sexually-orientated movies. These put you in a certain frame of mind and mood.

- Call your parents when you get to your destination and when you are on your way home. This saves them unnecessary worry.

- Stick to the curfew. Get back home at the appropriate time.

- Try not to spend too much time together. See how best you can develop a friendship.

- Do not become too serious in the relationship too soon.

- Feel free to date other people before making a decision.

- Do not allow yourself to be abused in any kind of way without reporting it or getting out of the relationship.

NOTES:

Note to self never
read Dating and piriod.
Again!

NOTES:

_____

_____

_____

_____

_____

_____

_____

_____

_____

_____

_____

_____

_____

_____

_____

_____

_____

_____

_____

_____

_____

NOTES:

NOTES:

TO CONTACT
PATRICE M. ELLIS, WRITE:

Mount Tabor Full Gospel Baptist Church
P.O. Box N-9705
Nassau, N.P., Bahamas

or

patriceellis2@yahoo.com
patriceellis@teiibahamas.com

For additional copies of this book, contact:

Tel: (242) 392-0708
or
(242) 392-9332